PLEAD YOUR CASE

By Kenneth E. Hagin

Chapter 1
PLEAD YOUR CASE

I, even I, am he that blotteth out thy transgressions for mine own sake, and will not remember thy sins.

Put me in remembrance: let us plead together: declare thou [set forth thy cause], that thou mayest be justified.

— Isaiah 43:25,26

Someone said, "It is more important that men learn to pray than to gain a college education." Notice he did not say that a college education is not important. He said learning to pray is more important. People go to great effort and expense to gain a college education. We may have to go to some effort, but it won't be expensive to learn to pray.

I feel so sorry for people who don't know how to pray when the crises of life come. They know how to say words, but just spouting words off into the atmosphere isn't praying — there is a vast difference.

In the 18th chapter of Genesis, we find Abraham praying:

GENESIS 18:23-25
23 And Abraham drew near, and said, Wilt thou also destroy the righteous with the wicked?
24 Peradventure there be fifty righteous within the city: wilt thou also destroy and not spare the place for the fifty righteous that are therein?
25 That be far from thee to do after this manner, to slay the righteous with the wicked: and that the righteous should be as the wicked, that be far from thee: Shall not the Judge of all the earth do right?

Prayer is joining forces with God the Father. It is fellowshipping with Him. It is carrying out His will upon the earth.

John Wesley, founder of Methodism, said, "It seems like God is limited by our prayer life. He can do nothing for humanity unless someone asks Him to do it."

You might ask, "Why is this?" You see, God made the world and the fullness thereof. Then He made man and gave man dominion over all the works of His hands. Adam was the god of this world. Adam, however, committed high treason and sold out to Satan, and Satan became the god of this world. He is called that in the New Testament (2 Cor. 4:4).

God doesn't just move in on top of Satan. If He did this, Satan could accuse Him of doing the same thing he did. But God devised a plan of salvation and sent His Son, the Lord Jesus Christ, whom Satan could not and did not touch. Through Jesus, God redeemed mankind! Now authority has been restored to us through Jesus Christ, and when we ask God, He can move! That is why it seems He can do nothing unless someone asks Him to.

Here in Genesis, God refused to destroy Sodom and Gomorrah until He had talked it over with Abraham, His blood covenant friend. Abraham's prayer is one of the most suggestive and illuminating prayers of the Old Testament. Abraham was taking his place in the covenant that God had made with him . . . the Old Testament . . . the old covenant.

Abraham had, through the covenant, received rights and privileges which we understand very little. The covenant Abraham had just solemnized with the Lord, Jehovah, gave him a legal standing with God. Therefore, we hear him speaking so plainly as he intercedes for Sodom and Gomorrah, *"Shall not the Judge of all the earth do right?"*

All through the Old Testament we find men who understood and took their place in the covenant. Joshua could open the Jordan. He could command the sun, moon, and stars to stand still in the heavens. Elijah could bring fire out of heaven to consume the altar as well as the sacrifice. David's mighty men were utterly shielded from death in time of war as long as they remembered the covenant. When you read of them in the Old Testament, you think you're reading about "Supermen." Practically all the prayers of the Old Testament are prayers of covenant men. They *had* to be answered. God *had* to give heed to their petitions.

Now let's discuss praying under the new covenant. The believer today has covenant rights, just as those in the Old Testament had covenant rights. In fact, the Bible says we have a *better* covenant established upon *better* promises (Heb. 8:6). We ought to be able to do all they did and more because we have a new covenant, a better covenant, established upon greater promises.

Chapter 2
ACCEPT THE CHALLENGE

Here is the challenge from a covenant-keeping God to Israel. It also is a challenge to the Church:

ISAIAH 43:25,26
25 I, even I, am he that blotteth out thy transgressions for mine own sake, and will not remember thy sins.
26 Put me in remembrance: let us plead together: declare thou, that thou mayest be justified.

First, God says, "I, even I, am He who blotteth out your transgressions, and will not remember your sins."

God does not remember that you have ever done anything wrong, so why should *you* remember it? If you can come to the Lord without a sense of sin-consciousness, you can come with faith and boldness and get your prayer heard and answered. Do you see what confidence that gives you? As long as you come under condemnation and with a sense of spiritual inferiority, you are going to come tongue-tied and fear-filled, and you won't get anywhere.

God said, "I will not remember thy sins." He has no knowledge that you have ever done anything wrong (provided you have been born again and provided that since becoming a child of God when you have failed you have confessed it). We are told in the New Testament, *"If we confess our sins, he is faithful and just to forgive us our sins, and to cleanse us from all unrighteousness"* (1 John 1:9).

Many people say when praying to receive the Holy Spirit or to receive healing, "I don't know if the Lord will hear me. I've failed. I'm such a failure." Well, He doesn't know you are a failure, so don't tell Him. He plainly said here, *"I will not remember your sins."* He does not remember that you have done anything wrong, so why should you remind Him of it? It is not good taste to remind Him. To remind Him that you have done wrong is to accuse Him of being a liar. He does not remember, so don't you remember. Then with confidence you can come before the throne of grace!

Second, He said, *"Put me in remembrance."* What does He mean by that? In other words, we are to remind Him of His promises in regard to prayer. When you pray, stand before the throne of God, remind Him of His promises, lay your case legally before Him, and plead it as a lawyer. A lawyer is continually bringing up law and precedent. You bring His Word — His covenant promises. He said here, *"Put me in remembrance: let us plead together: declare thou* [or as the margin of the *King James Version* says, 'Set forth thy cause'], *that thou mayest be justified."* God is asking you to bring His Word, to put Him in remembrance. He is asking you to plead your covenant rights. Here is a challenge from God to lay your case before Him. If your children are unsaved or whatever it is you are praying about, find the Scripture that covers your case and lay the matter before Him.

Be definite. Find the Scriptures that definitely promise you those things you need. When we come according to God's Word, God's Word does not fail.

Chapter 3
STAND ON HIS WORD

. . . Ask me of things to come concerning my sons, and concerning the work of my hands command ye me.

— Isaiah 45:11

This Scripture is prophetic and quite startling. It does not apply to Israel. It is yours. Israelites were *servants* of God. We are *sons* (1 John 3:2). This verse in Isaiah has reference to us, and it is in perfect harmony with the following Scripture from the New Testament.

JOHN 15:7
7 If ye abide in me, and my words abide in you, ye shall ask what ye will, and it shall be done unto you.

You do not command in tones of arrogance, but as a partner — a worker together with Him — you lay the case before Him. You call His attention to His part in the drama of life.

ISAIAH 55:9-11

9 For as the heavens are higher than the earth, so are my ways higher than your ways, and my thoughts than your thoughts.

10 For as the rain cometh down, and the snow from heaven, and returneth not thither, but watereth the earth, and maketh it bring forth and bud, that it may give seed to the sower, and bread to the eater:

11 So shall my word be that goeth forth out of my mouth: it shall not return unto me void, but it shall accomplish that which I please, and it shall prosper in the thing whereto I sent it.

The eleventh verse is a Scripture you should continually use in prayer. It is the very backbone of the prayer life. No word that has gone forth from God can return unto Him void.

God said, "... *I will hasten my word to perform it*" (Jer. 1:12). The margin of the *King James Version* reads, "I will watch over my word to perform it."

He will make His Word good if you dare stand on it!

Chapter 4
PRACTICAL APPLICATIONS

I followed this procedure exactly in an experience you may have heard me relate before.

In the last church I pastored, the Sunday School superintendent, a pumper in the East Texas oil fields, fell off the engine house down into the machinery.

As I drove through town, someone stopped me and said, "Did you know that Brother Haynes is dead?"

I said, "No, he isn't dead. I was just out on the lease fifteen minutes ago talking to him."

"Well, after you left, he climbed up on the engine house and fell down into the machinery, and he is dead."

I hurried back to the lease and made my way through the crowd to the engine house, where Brother Haynes lay on the ground. I knelt beside him.

Dr. Garret, the physician who had been summoned, said to me, "Reverend Hagin, I thought he was dead; however, he isn't quite dead yet. But he is dying. He will never regain consciousness. We can't move him; he will die lying right here. I wish you would take Mrs. Haynes aside and prepare her."

I took Sister Haynes by the arm to lead her to one side, but before I could say a word to her she said, "Dr. Garret doesn't think Daddy will live, does he?"

"No, he doesn't," I answered.

She looked up and smiled through her tears and said, "Isn't it wonderful that you and I have 'inside information'?"

I said, "It surely is!"

We prayed. He kept on living.

The ambulance waited about an hour and a half. Finally, Dr. Garret said, "Well, let's try to get him to the hospital. I didn't think he would live this long."

I rode in the ambulance with him to the hospital, some thirty miles away. Three specialists were waiting when we arrived.

To make a long story short, we had been there two days and were facing the third night when one of the doctors said to me, "Reverend, I will tell you the truth about it, we don't even know the extent of his injuries, because we can't move him. How he has lived this long, we don't know. We do know his left lung is deflated; however, we don't know what internal injuries and hemorrhaging he may have. He is still in shock, and we can't bring him out. There is no chance of his making it."

Sister Haynes' faith was slipping. When you sit with a person over a period of hours and grow tired physically, it is easy for your spirit and your faith to be affected. So I knew I had to get her out of her husband's hospital room, and I did.

This was the third night I had been up with very little sleep, and at about 2 o'clock in the morning, I began to fall asleep. The special nurse awakened me as she stirred around the bed. The way she looked, I asked her if Brother Haynes was dead, and she replied, "I thought he was, but he isn't quite yet. I know I'm not supposed to talk this way to you, but he will never make it till 7 o'clock in the morning when my shift ends."

I got up and went out into the corridor, and at 2 o'clock in the morning in that hospital, I did just exactly what I suggest you do. I did just exactly what God said to do. He said, *"Put me in remembrance."* He said, *"Let us plead together."* He said, *"Set forth thy cause that thou mayest be justified."*

So I said to the Lord, "Lord, I am not going to let him die. First of all, he is only 49 years old, and a man 49 years old is not old enough to die."

I reminded Him, "You promised us in Your Word at least 70 or 80 years.

"Second, he is our Sunday School superintendent. He usually endeavors to visit every absentee himself. He is really the best Sunday School superintendent I have ever had in all of the churches I have pastored. There is not another man like-minded in our church. This isn't my church; it is Your church. I am the under-shepherd, but You are the Great Shepherd. What I need, You need. I need him.

"Third, He is my deacon. He always stands solidly with me, and all the other men follow him. I need him. If I need him, You need him.

"Fourth, he has influence for good in our town. The businessmen and practically everyone in the city have more confidence in him than in all the rest of the men put together. I need him.

"Fifth, he gives 30 percent of his income to the church. If we lose that, we will be almost bankrupt. I know You can meet every need, but your ways of meeting needs are through men."

(God is not going to rain money down out of heaven. He is not a counterfeiter. God's way of doing things is through men. Remember that Jesus said in Luke 6:38, *"Give, and it shall be given unto you; good measure, pressed down, and shaken together, and running over, shall men give into your bosom . . . . "* Shall *men* give.)

So I said, "This is not my church. We are the Body of Christ. You are the Head. What the Body needs, the Head needs. Lord, we need him. The church needs him, and so I am not going to let him die.

"Besides that, death is of the enemy. It is of the devil." (Death is an enemy. It is not of God. Death is the last enemy that shall be put under foot, the Bible says. However, God has taken the sting out of death for us.)

I said, "I rebuke death and I command it

to leave his body in the Name of the Lord Jesus Christ of Nazareth."

I went back into the room. Brother Haynes was breathing well and his color looked good. The nurse was reading a magazine. I sat down, became sleepy again, and fell off to sleep. The special nurse awakened me as she moved about. When I first looked at Brother Haynes, I thought, "My, I have gone to sleep and let the devil come in here and take him, and he has died." I got up and went through the same procedure again. I argued my case the same way. I did that the third time before he rested well.

At 8 o'clock the doctor came in. The moment he listened to his heart, he said, "Nurse, get the stretcher. We are going to take him to X-ray." He turned to me and said, "This man has come out of it. He is out of shock. He might make it now." Thank God, he did make it!

When he came back to church, he testified. (I had never told him or anyone how I had prayed.) He said, "Folks, don't ever feel sorry for Christians who die. The last thing I remember was falling. I never remember hitting the machinery. The next thing I knew I woke up in the hospital. They tell me it was several days. It seemed like only a few minutes. When I did wake up, I never did hurt. I never had any pain. It was most amazing.

"The only thing I can remember while I was unconscious is that I must have died. I went up to heaven, and I saw the angels. I heard them sing: oh, such singing as you have never heard! I saw the saints robed in white. I stood among them, and I saw Jesus. He came to me.

"I was just about to fall down before Him to tell Him how much I love and appreciate Him when He pointed His finger at me and said, 'You're going to have to go back.' I said, 'I don't want to go back.' Again He pointed His finger at me and said, 'You are going to have to go back.' I said, 'I don't want to go back.' He said the third time, 'You are going to have to go back to the earth.' And I said the third time, 'I don't want to go back to the earth.'

"He reached around as a person would if he were standing by a window. It seemed that He pulled back a curtain, and when He did, I heard Brother Hagin say, 'Lord, I'm not going to let him die. I'm not going to let him die.'

"Jesus said, 'See, you are going to have to go back. Brother Hagin won't let you come yet.' "

(I always have believed we have more authority than we think we have!)

I stood before the throne and pled my case like a lawyer. Praise God, we can! We have Scripture for it: *"Put me in remembrance,"* God said. *"Let us plead together: declare thou, that you may be justified."*

In 1950 my father-in-law had an operation. He never had asked anyone to pray for his healing, but he asked me to pray with him, and I did. Nineteen days after the operation, he was still in the hospital. Complications had set in.

My mother-in-law had stayed with him night and day. When she saw that he wasn't going to make it, she had a nervous collapse. My wife had gone home with her. I was there with him, and he was unconscious.

Incidentally, the Lord revealed to me exactly what was happening to him physically. I mentioned this to the doctor, and he looked at me in amazement and said, "How did you know that? That is exactly what is happening to him, but a person would not know that unless he were medically trained." I am glad the Lord knows everything!

As I stood there I prayed quietly to myself (as were others in the room), "Lord, do You want me to curse this death and command it to go? Shall I command this sickness and physical condition to be made well? I believe I will just do it."

Immediately, the Lord said to me, "No, don't do it!"

(Notice the text says, *"Let us plead together."* You can talk to Him, and He will talk to you.)

The Lord began to plead *His* case. He said, "Now he is 70 years old. He is ready to go. He hasn't always been ready to go, but he is now. He has all of his business settled. Financially, materially, spiritually — everything is ready. He never will have a better time to go than now. You leave him alone and let him go."

Immediately, I replied, "All right, Lord, on one condition: You let him come out of this death and leave a good testimony, and I'll let him go."

I had not gotten those words out till he opened his eyes. He looked at me and said, "Kenneth."

I said, "Yes sir, Mr. Rooker."

He said, "I'm dying."

I said, "I know."

"The sooner the better," he said. "I know what I'm doing now."

The doctor said afterwards, "I would not have believed that if another doctor had told me. If I had not seen it with my own eyes, I would not have believed it." He gave me some medical term. He said that he wasn't exactly dead, and he wasn't exactly alive, but about halfway between the two. He told me he had never seen anybody come back when they were out that far.

That night we had a great time. Mr. Rooker sat up in bed, and we brought our children in. He sat up and laughed and talked, and you would have thought he was going on a vacation the next day. He kissed those grandchildren — the only ones he had — goodbye without a tear.

The next afternoon at about the same time he had regained consciousness, he become unconscious again. I knew that when death fastened its final throes upon him, he would regain consciousness momentarily, because I had been there several times myself.

When he came to that point, I saw that look of consciousness flash across his face. He quickly fastened his eyes on me and said, "Kenneth, I'm dying."

I said, "I know, Mr. Rooker, but you are not afraid."

"No, I'm not afraid."

"Just lie back on the pillow and let her go."

He just lay back, bless God, and went to sleep. A smile flickered across his face, and he went to be with Jesus.

He had told me the night he had regained consciousness, "There has been a man right up there for the last two days. Every now and then he will motion to me to come on."

He had said to the angel, "Sir, I don't rightly know who you are, but I'm not quite ready yet. You will have to wait a little while."

I still believe that we have more authority

than we have ever used upon the earth.

God said, *"Let us plead together."* There may be times you will plead with God and He will plead with you. You can see that this was the best way to handle Mr. Rooker's case. God did answer my prayer: Mr. Rooker came out of it immediately, and he left a good testimony.

PSALM 78:41
41 Yea, they turned back and tempted God, and limited the Holy One of Israel.

Can you limit God? The Bible says that Israel limited Him. The marginal rendering reads, "And they turned again and tempted God and limited the Holy One of Israel."

We have limited Him. We have limited Him with our prayer life. We have let the great promises of fellowship and cooperation with God go by untouched and unrealized. But, thank God, we can act upon His Word.

Chapter 5
NEW TESTAMENT
PRAYER PROMISES

Verily I say unto you, Whatsoever ye shall bind on earth shall be bound in heaven: and whatsoever ye shall loose on earth shall be loosed in heaven.

Again I say unto you, That if two of you shall agree on earth as touching any thing that they shall ask, it shall be done for them of my Father which is in heaven.

For where two or three are gathered together in my name, there am I in the midst of them.
— Matthew 18:18-20

This Scripture is amazing! ". . . Where two or three are gathered together in my name, there am I"!

We often quote this verse in regard to a church service. It has no reference to a church service. However, it is true the Lord is there. He is saying that wherever two believers agree, He is right there with them. That would be an executive meeting, so to speak, with the

Master. We come together to do business — sitting in His presence, planning, discussing, and then praying. For He said, *"if two of you shall agree...."* Unless you do some planning and discussing, you won't know what you are agreeing on.

The group may be small: perhaps just a husband and wife. But if they agree as touching anything they ask, it shall be done. *It shall be done!* This is a challenge!

We never have fathomed the depth of what this Scripture can mean to us. And we will not until we act upon it.

Where two agree in prayer, the power of the two increases tenfold over one. The Bible says that one shall put a thousand to flight, but two will put ten thousand (Deut. 32:30). You can be mighty in prayer alone, but you can be mightier in prayer united or joined together with someone else. Every "believer" should find an "agreer" — someone to join with him or her in prayer.

We should lay out a program of prayer, making a list of subjects and of people to lay intelligently before God the Father.

JOHN 15:7,8

7 If you abide in me, and my words abide in you, ye shall ask what ye will, and it shall be done unto you.

8 Herein is my Father glorified, that ye bear much fruit; so shall ye be my disciples.

"If ye abide in me..." If we are born again, we do abide in Him. If He had just said that and that alone, we would have had it made. But He adds, *"...AND my Words abide in you..."* His Word abides in us in the measure that it governs our lives — in the measure that we act upon it.

If His Words abide in us, we are bound to have faith, because the Bible says, *"So then faith cometh by hearing, and hearing by the word of God"* (Rom. 10:17). It would be an impossibility for His Word to abide in us and for us not to have faith. Unbelief (or doubt) is a result of ignorance of the Word of God.

If we are living the Word, then when we come to pray, that Word dwells in us so richly that it will become His Word on our lips. It will be as the Father's words were on the lips of the Master, Jesus.

JOHN 15:16
16 Ye have not chosen me, but I have chosen you,
and ordained you, that ye should go and bring forth
fruit, and that your fruit should remain: that whatsoever ye shall ask of the Father in my name, he may
give it you.

JOHN 16:23,24
23 And in that day ye shall ask me nothing. Verily,
verily, I say unto you, Whatsoever ye shall ask the
Father in my name, he will give it you.
24 Hitherto have ye asked nothing in my name: ask,
and ye shall receive, that your joy may be full.

Prayer is addressed to the Father in Jesus'
Name. This is divine order. And this statement,
"... *whatsoever ye shall ask of the Father in
my name, he may give it you,*" has within it the
ability to bring God into our circumstances, our
families, our homes, our nation or whatever it
is that we are praying about.

We are not praying to Jesus. We are praying
to the Father in the Name of Jesus. That's the
way Jesus said to do it.

You can fellowship with the Master and talk
things over with Him. But when it comes to

prayer based on legal grounds, it is to be addressed to the Father in the Name of Jesus.

Jesus really gives us the power of attorney. That means that what Jesus can do, we can do. That means that Jesus' Name gives us the right to go into the presence of the Father God and receive answers to our prayers. Jesus backs our prayers! He makes them good.

1 JOHN 5:14,15

14 And this is the confidence [boldness] that we have in him, that, if we ask any thing according to his will, he heareth us:

15 And if we know that he hear us, whatsoever we ask, we know that we have the petitions that we desired of him.

The believer, walking in fellowship with the Word, never will ask for anything outside of the Father's will (outside of the Word). We need not worry about that. (If the believer is not walking in fellowship with the Father, or with the Word, he is not going to get anything anyway.)

You see, friends, we can find out God's will in the Bible, for it is His will, His covenant, His testament. It is His will for us to have what He has provided, what He has purchased, what He has bought.

We know that saving the lost is His will — for this end He died. We do not pray, "God, save my mother who is lost — if it is your will. Don't let her go to hell — if it is your will. If it is not your will, let her go on to hell." No! Why don't we pray that way? Because we read in God's will, His Word — *"For God so loved the world, that he gave his only begotten Son, that whosoever believeth in him should not perish, but have everlasting life"* (John 3:16).

We know that saving the lost is God's will, because the Bible also says, *"The Lord is not . . . willing that any should perish, but that all should come to repentance"* (2 Peter 3:9). Saving the lost is His will.

We know that healing the sick is His will, because God's Word tells us, *"Who his own self bare our sins in his own body on the tree, that we, being dead to sins, should live unto righteousness: by whose stripes ye were healed"* (1 Peter 2:24). And because His Word says, *". . . Himself took our infirmities, and bare our sicknesses"* (Matt. 8:17). It is God's will that we have what Jesus bought for us.

We know that praying for finances to meet obligations is God's will, according to Philippians 4:19, *"But my God shall supply all your need according to his riches in glory by Christ Jesus."* In this fourth chapter of Philippians he is talking about finances.

It is His will that our needs be met. God said to Israel, *"If ye be willing and obedient, ye shall eat the good of the land"* (Isa. 1:19). Of course, you can't walk in disobedience and enjoy the good things of God. But if you are willing and obedient, God wants you to have the best. He is not a miser or a tightwad. He didn't put everything here for the devil and his crowd.

Some people have the idea that you should never have anything financially or materially if you are a Christian — that you should go through life with your nose to the grindstone.

Jesus said, *"If ye then, being evil, know how to give good gifts unto your children, how much more shall your Father which is in heaven give good things to them that ask him?"* (Matt. 7:11).

Oh, He wants to. He wants to. But people won't cooperate with Him and let Him.

How many of you parents desire that your children go through life sick and afflicted, down-trodden, down-and-out, poverty-stricken, nose to the grindstone? None of you!

Jesus said, "*If ye then, being evil, know how to give good gifts unto your children, HOW MUCH MORE....*" How much more! He wants us to have the best. God wants us to prosper and have the good things of this life.

No, He does not want us to be covetous. That is wrong. In fact, the Lord said to me once, as He sat down by my bedside and talked to me for an hour and a half, "My Spirit will lead all of my children. The Bible says that as many as are led by the Spirit, they are the sons God, and the Spirit leads by an inward witness. I will lead you and not only you, but any child of God.

"I will show you what to do with your money. I will show you how to invest it. In fact, if you will listen to me, I will make you rich. I am not opposed to my children being rich. I am opposed to their being covetous."

Someone could be covetous and not have a

dime. Some misread and say, "Money is the root of all evil." The Bible does not say that. It says, *"For the love of money is the root of all evil. . . ."* (1 Tim. 6:10). It is all right to have money. It is wrong for money to have you.

We can pray that ministers will speak in the power of the Spirit. We can pray for the lost in heathen lands. All this is in His will.

What boldness we have, then, to come to God. This is the confidence that we have in Him: that if we ask anything according to His will, He hears us. (All of these things are according to His will, so we know that when we pray about them, He hears us.) And we KNOW if He hears us, we KNOW we have the petition we ask of Him. We KNOW we have it! We KNOW it! Praise God!

MARK 11:24
24 Therefore I say unto you, What things soever ye desire, when ye pray, believe that ye receive them, and ye shall have them.

MATTHEW 21:21,22
21 Jesus answered and said unto them, Verily I say

unto you, If ye have faith, and doubt not, ye shall not only do this which is done to the fig tree, but also if ye shall say unto this mountain, Be thou removed, and be thou cast into the sea; it shall be done.
22 And all things, whatsoever ye shall ask in prayer, believing, ye shall receive.

Believe it first; then you shall have it. If you believe you have something, you are going to thank God for it.

Faith actually is thanking God for something you possess that has not yet materialized. However, you know it is yours and you possess it without seeing it.

MARK 9:23
23 Jesus said unto him, If thou canst believe, all things are possible to him that believeth.

All things — all things — are possible to the man who cooperates with the Lord, who fellowships with the Lord, who is a co-laborer of the Lord.